On [things & stuff]

By LMB Wordsmith
(Chief No Feathers)

On [things & stuff]

Table of Contents

On Existence

The puppies and I had a fire going near our garden one evening. It was a rubbish fire of odds and ends, sticks and leaves, cleaning the garden of its winter debris, making it ready for a new year's growth.

I turned from watching the puppies play to watching the fire with its changing forms and its lively dance of colors. As I stood there a moth came by and circled the fire.

Circling the fire, the moth wound its way down the side. Below the flaming leaves and rubbish were some logs, glowing bright, intense. Too hot for flames; no flames but heat. And bright.

The moth shot in.

Its wings shriveled. It fell,

crippled,

on to a glowing coal.

Its body bubbled –

And vanished.

I looked, but there was only a glowing coal.

The drop had become a speck, and then – gone.

Vaporized.

The moth – was that what I had seen?

It was gone, but . . .

I looked again, but there was nothing there but a glowing coal.

Not a trace existed to tell me if the moth had ever flown,

had ever lived,

had ever been.

I looked,

But saw nothing.

I thought,

And I thought I remembered . . .

a moth.

But.

A quiver ran through my body – a queer thing to happen by a fire.

The Spark Of Life

There are things I don't understand.

Actually, there are a lot of things I don't understand.

I can see – but I still don't understand.

One of them is the Spark of Life – the Spark that is missing from the corpse, but was quite evident a moment earlier when the person was alive and smiling and talking to you.

The mass of cells, the conglomeration of muscle, bones and flesh remain the same[1] – only the Spark is gone.

*****

I learned when I was young that there is a difference between life and death.

There is no "replay" or "reset" button. We can't try to do it differently this next time. There is no "next time".

When the life ended, the Spark was out, and that chapter was closed (but see on the other hand Billy Mitchell in "**& THAT**, My Friends, Is Tactical Surprise!").

I saw it with my grandfather, and then about two years later with my dad, when I studied their faces in the open caskets at their funerals.

There was something markedly different with both of them, from how I knew them in life to how they looked in the casket.

The only thought or word that came to mind – the only difference – was a Spark. One moment the Spark existed, and the next moment the Spark was gone.

What happened to, and where did my dad and grandpa go?

& where did their Sparks go?

---

[1] See, e.g., <u>Einstein's Brain</u> in "When Times Were Bad".

Emotion

What is it?

You can't feel it in your hands, taste it with your tongue, or see it with your eyes.

On a scale, it won't even move a needle.

It binds some of us together – but makes others mutual and deadly enemies.

It includes some as within the circle – and others as outcasts.

So when I come across a hearse coming in the opposite direction followed by perhaps fifty limousines and cars, I suspect: ~ Well, some stranger has over 100 people who knew him. Depending upon the road and the section of the country I observe this, we: (a) either all pull over to the side of the road in respect for this stranger, or (b) whizz on by the opposing traffic.

> [Though I've heard of some down here who go to the funeral –
>
>> To view the corpse in the open casket;
>> Who then follow the hearse along with another 50 or so vehicles;
>> To hear the last prayer by the preacher by the graveside;
>> To watch the casket being lowered into the grave;
>>   & shovelfuls of dirt being thrown on top of the casket . . .
>
>> – just to be sure the ol' bastard is dead!]

It's taken awhile for me, but I've begun to see and understand that puppies have personalities and emotions too – just like pigs and people [just better and nicer]. [President Harry Truman saw this also when he observed: ~ If you want a friend in Washington [the capital of the United States of America] – get a dog!]

I can see this when a puppy spots me from across the cabin and comes running toward me, unable to contain his joy: his tail is wagging fiercely; his body is wagging fiercely. I can't tell if his tail is wagging his body or his body is wagging the tail – to me, they are all wagging together uncontrollably.

On the other hand, there is coy Little Miss Bella: she lies on her favorite rug pretending to be napping, pretending to be ignoring me – but her fabulous white tail is wagging furiously, unmasking the pretense she is trying so desperately to maintain.

Yet when I hold one of my puppies who is in convulsive fits, or whose eye has just been punctured by the fangs of a poisonous snake, I break down, cry, and hold and cuddle my baby.

There is something very strange, very weird, about this thing which weighs nothing but can bring you down like a ton of bricks or can lift you to the heavens or allows you to soar with the eagles.

Emotion: What is it?

Dresden

Europe had for centuries, and if we are still lucky, still has, an interesting form of education called the "Continental Education". It consisted of traveling to foreign countries, the idea being that travel in and of itself to other cultures and other peoples can be an education.

My school embraced this concept in its "Semester Abroad" programs[2] so we had 3 ½ days of classes each week and 3 ½ days during which we were to travel on our own. We also had several group trips, one of which took us behind The Iron Curtain when the Cold War was almost hot: the United States was in the midst of the Vietnam War (which Russia and China kept out of ["officially"] while supplying all the arms and munitions used by North Vietnam[3]) and Russia still had tanks in Wenceslaus Square following its brutal suppression of The Prague Spring in 1968.

The Bridge to Wenceslaus Square in Prague.

It also, of course, had tanks all along the line that constituted the "Iron Curtain". [As we were told soon after arriving in Southern Germany: just realize, you are only an hour by tank from the Iron Curtain (when I later moved to Alaska, I was informed: just think, you are only 5 minutes by missile from Russia).]

---

[2] See "Nestor".

[3] See "When You Win By Losing".

The Germans had been bloody and ruthless in their invasion of Russia in World War II. The Russians didn't see any need to be otherwise when the tide turned and they were able to invade Germany from the east. So even though 25 years had passed since the end of WW II, the only thing Russia had done in Dresden was simply bulldoze the rubble to the side of the streets. They hadn't bothered with trying to remove the rubble.

This poem was originally written about the bombing of Hamburg, but was written after I had seen Dresden. One aspect of nuclear weapons is that they cause "fire-storms", where, because of the intense heat generated, there is not enough air (oxygen) near the fire for the fire to burn – so to get the air the fire needs, air is brought in by violent winds from the countryside . . . so people and debris are <u>sucked into</u> the fire.

"Fire-storms" are not limited however to nuclear weapons – if the right mixture is used [which the Allies knew of], they can be created by conventional bombs, as was done on Dresden, Hamburg and Tokyo (and with higher death totals than either Hiroshima or Nagasaki)[4].

____

[4] I am quite aware that it is fashionable now to be against the dropping of the A-Bombs on Hiroshima or Nagasaki. It is nice to be fashionable – you don't have to deal with reality.

But in the calculus of war, 70,000 dead Japanese is better than over 500,000 dead American Marines and Soldiers [and more if Paratroopers like Henry are brought into consideration (see "Henry (Brains, Guts & Charm)")] if an invasion of the Japanese Home Islands had gone on as planned (<u>plus another 200,000 Allied POW's</u> who the Empire of Japan had vowed to execute immediately upon such an invasion).

Yet further, for reasons I have not been able to fathom [possibly because they don't exist], people who argue that the A-Bombs should not have been dropped think that if they hadn't been dropped, that these 70,000 people would still be alive. What they don't understand is that if these 70,000 were still alive . . . the War would still be going on!

And if the War was still going on, these 70,000 Japanese would be <u>minuscule</u> compared to the 7,000,000 to 15,000,000 dead Japanese that were likely to have died in such a fight for the Home Islands if the Atom Bombs had not been dropped.

It is also <u>minor</u> compared to the number of babies and kids that would have been thrown over cliffs to their deaths by their Japanese parents [before they jumped over the cliffs themselves] – <u>just like thousands</u> had done on Saipan <u>a year earlier</u>.

> *[This phenomenon of throwing babies off cliffs by their own parents was not then known to the American or Western mind.]*

But Japanese women realized this all too well back in 1945, even if modern American Presidents do not.

> [As an example, when the invasion of England was imminent (during the Battle of Britain in 1940) by the Germans, the English didn't throw their babies over the White Cliffs of Dover – they packed their kids in trains and sent them out to the countryside to survive and so that there would be another generation for the future.

> This was most obviously antithetical, or at least diametrically opposed, to what the Japanese parents did 4 years later on the island of Saipan.]   [cont.]

The statue of Martin Luther, blackened but otherwise unscathed, survived the Dresden Bombing and Firestorm.

Marienkirche (St. Mary's Church) [the rubble behind him] did not.

[footnote cont.]

Of course, it all could have been averted if the Japanese had not attacked Pearl Harbor first (please see "John Paul Jones – Where Art Thou?" in this regard).

And the war may not have actually ended with Hiroshima or Nagasaki anyway – see "Dulles International Airport" – just the tactics and the weapons.

Further, the <u>nature of man</u> is often <u>overlooked</u> in these discussions: if the A-Bombs had <u>not</u> been used in World War II, it is <u>almost certain</u> they would have been used, and <u>in greater numbers</u>, in the next war. It may be remembered that in fact during the next war that General Douglas MacArthur wanted to initially use about a dozen nuclear weapons on Red China during the Korean War. But President Harry Truman, having authorized the first use of nuclear weapons, and seeing its effects, nixed the idea and fired General MacArthur instead.

The Wreckage Wrought

Across the square from the cathedral stood the statue of a war-hero. Blackened from the night-time bombings, but still astride his horse, he waved his upraised sword victorious over the conquered debris.

In front the rubble had been bulldozed into a pile, and over their blackened, jagged edges a troupe of boys played "King of the Mountain". And up in the air the unfelled walls hovered precariously above the romping children, standing from habit only it seems for their buttresses lay amongst the heap.

    – It had taken seventy-five years to build

      (but only one night to destroy).

I looked at the rubble, jagged and scraped where once it'd been polished. It laid there in the side street littering the ground and blocking the way, unmolested by peace. I took a step, but could not go on; the wreckage wrought would not let me by.

waves of bombers and illuminating flares

    brighten the heavenly sky

    bringing day before the night has fled

    sounds and lights awaken the lovers

mighty thunder and little cracks, screaming lights and flashing sirens

    arouse the children from their slumber

crashing chandeliers screeching cats

    spilt goldfish and fractured china

    broken toys and shattered glass

gashed bodies gushing blood

thrown from their beds

   stumbling into lurching walls

   falling through missing steps

people and walls collide

blood oozes

through the crack

down the wall

crumbling buildings crash in shock

burning embers cut the sky

fiery meteors light the night

sirens

twisted limbs and broken bodies

leap amongst the flames

fall amidst the fires

burning wood and burning bodies

are but burning bits of carbon

thunder bombs

thud dully, boringly, deadly

over the local charnel

polished marble singed by flames

undercut by discord

totters above the altar

crashes upon the crucifix

asunder torn

splintered tiles wrenched apart

rain through the rupture

snow upon the tabernacle

polished marble to bruin boulders

art to ashes

beauty banished

dissipated life evaporated death

A dud

explodes

shredding a young woman

into bloody confetti

to baptize the passing child

bubbling intestines

molten flesh

broil together

in the percolating tar

a stray dog

sniffs the human waste

relieves himself

on the human meat

blood

mixing with the street oil

gathers the city's dirt

cleans the travelled pavement

down the alleyway

to the marketplace

sewers collect the refuse

dumping it in the river

ruptured veins

of water burst

gushing forth

in lustrous fountains

spraying people

cats

and cars

painting them in vibrant colors

sparkling in the moonlight

gleaming in the starlight

glistening in the firelight

they stand

dazzled by the glitter

water

relief

streams down the gutter

bloody corpses and broken bikes

litter the street

rats scatter by shattered glass

tinkling the debris

stranded unattended

a baby carriage waits

magnesium bombs enrapture the asphalt in flames

cooks the human meat

sizzling in the street

dancing shadows

& leaping flames

beguile & belinger

the bogus shapes and the fearful chimera

fumes of asphalt, stench of flesh

arise together

commingle

vorx betwixt flames and burning debris

aspire as one

excelsior

the community of saints

gather in mass

the community of corpses

from the rusty nail

blood

drips

*****

A tree in Scotland that started life handicapped – upside-down!, but with the force of Mother Nature turned itself around and stands upright and strong.

from the rubble grows a flower

on an obscure wall it blossoms

unmindful of the past

in peace content with now

On Time

Leading Minds

*****

I used to think that if one understood another's concept of Time, one had the key to understanding everything else of importance about that other person's concept of life and the Universe.

[All we EACH have, EVERY ONE, is Time.

Some among us may also have money, some land, and others prestige or heritage.

And yet others have: [nothing].

BUT we all have Time: limited, fleeting, ephemeral, and in the end finite.

*Till then, **THAT** is all we have in common.]*

*****

[Section I is for adults to help them think about and understand "time", while Section II is for kids – to let them think and wonder.]

I

Ideas Regarding Time

We humans, at least those of us with sight, perceive what is about us in 3 dimensions. [A new "dimension" is 90 degrees from all other, previous, dimensions.] Our eyes and brains are wired to only go out 3 dimensions. In math, we go out to a 4th dimension: time.

*****

P.D. Ouspensky was a Russian mathematician in the early part of the 20th century. For me, he was difficult to read. I'm a slow reader anyway as I read each word and listen to the sound and cadence of a sentence or string of words. I tried to read Ouspensky several times, but had to give up. Then one day I picked up one of his books (<u>Tertium Organum</u>) [the first Organum (or "Whole", as in a complete, integrated thought of the Whole Universe) had been written by Aristotle, and the second one was by Francis Bacon], and something "clicked" – I was able to read it faster than nearly any other book in my life.

P.D. Ouspensky's mentor was G.I. Gurdjieff [for more on Gurdjieff, please see "W.A.R. & My Greek Tragedy Case"], a fellow Russian and a mystic. Over time, Ouspensky was able to mix and intertwine the Western <u>objective</u> viewpoint of mathematics with the Eastern <u>subjective</u> viewpoint of mystics.

*****

To set the stage here, Ouspensky developed a beautiful thought-picture:

He said imagine a snail [its walk across the earth being 1 dimension – the path it travelled] crossing a piece of paper [2 dimensions].

But if we put a line on the piece of paper, and the snail crossed it, the snail would experience nothing [before the line]; then something [the line itself]; and then nothing [after having crossed the line]. This "nothing-something-nothing" is what we perceive and call "time".

We, on the other hand, with our superior intelligence, know that the "line" is NOT time, but a 2nd dimension to the 1 dimensional life and path of the snail.

Ouspensky then jumped to the next dimension – using the analogy of a plane (2 dimensions) cutting through the upper branches of a tree. For those constrained to the 2 dimensional plane, they would see separate, unrelated circles and ovals (however the plane cut through the branches of the tree).

But we, with our superior intelligence, would know that these separate, unrelated circles and ovals were really of one organism: the tree itself [which is in 3 dimensions][5].

---

[5] See the Gum Trees in "Seeing Is Believing" after the pigs got through with eating all the dirt between "them".

After that, our organic brains fail, so Ouspensky went to analogy — with the whole of one life intertwining with other lives, with other beings, and with the Universe itself.

*****

For Sir Isaac Newton, time was fixed, constant, immutable, unchangeable.

A second or hour <u>here</u> was the same length of time as a second or hour <u>there</u>, as well as <u>back then</u> or sometime in the <u>future</u>.

It was a single, fixed constant.

It kept the Universe ordinary, knowable, and predictable.

*****

For Albert Einstein, however, time was a function of and changed with one's velocity through space.

At lower, slower, speeds, the perception of one of our current astronauts would be similar to his earth-bound observers. But if a future astronaut's velocity approached the speed of light, <u>time would slow</u> for him[6] [in relation to his earth-bound observer]. So (using Einstein's thought-picture involving twins), the one twin [the astronaut] would be speeding through the galaxies at nearly the speed of light and keeping his youth while his other twin, his brother back on earth, would be aging and dying. [When the astronaut brother returned to see his earth-bound twin, while he was still young and vigorous, his brother was now old, feeble and gray.]

Understanding Einstein's concept of time was therefore a wonderful entry into the rest of his thought.

*****

Then there is the surrealistic painter Salvador Dali. He didn't use words. He didn't use numbers. He just used images: his paintings are full of melting clocks and timepieces.

What does a melting clock mean?

What does it lead to or infer?

If you know, you might have a greater insight into Dali's work.

____

[6] A corollary regarding the speed of time [which Einstein did not investigate] is: that it appears that <u>time speeds up</u> as one gets older!

*****

And then there is this thought:

> Out of nothing, nothing comes
> Out of No-thing, everything becomes

And the No-thing – of which we are – is Now. Not in a past that is gone or a future that is not yet, but in the present which remains forever, forever moving – eternal. Not like a dot on a piece of paper, but like a stream in the forest, the present keeps moving, changing, in different forms it comes, with some things appearing and other things receding. Each moment is unique, and each is individual to itself. Tuesday is not the same as Monday, nor is five minutes on one day the same as five minutes on another. Yet, even after this, without the mind there would be no time, for time is known by the occurrence of events, and it is the discrimination between events that brings about the idea of time. But time is an artifice of the mind, real only in the world between men.

Time, the great divorcer, man's creation, has become his tyrant. But its tyranny continues only so long as he permits it to, and he'll permit it to so long as he believes it is independent of him. But when he realizes that time is rather dependent upon him for its existence, he can free himself from it.

Through the Now he passes from the temporal into the Eternal. Time, and its implications, can no longer harm him. Truly, his body shall rot beneath the sod, or its ashes shall be scattered by the winds, but he will have moved on. No, not even death can harm him – so what then can life do to him?

Good and bad are alike fictions of the mind. When one has transcended the relative world of opposites to become in harmony with the eternal flux in the moment, one's actions are right – neither good nor bad.

But let it be known that this knowledge is not knowledge that one can come upon as a stone, nor through effort reach.

This knowledge is inherent within oneself. Only there will one find it. Not to another can one look, nor that hopefully someday in the future it may come to pass that one might . . .. Anything outside oneself can only bring one to the threshold, but the critical thing is crossing it. That can only happen within. It's but one step, but it's a crucial one. It's like a polygon wanting to become a circle: no matter how many sides a polygon adds to itself, no matter how close it approximates a circle, it doesn't become one with it.

Only by leaving behind the nature of distinct sides, only when all the distinct sides become one side, does it become a circle. But that last step between the polygon and the circle cannot be made by adding just one more side. That gap cannot be bridged by one more step as before, but only by a leap out of the very nature to which it clings. Only then will it arrive, only then will multiplicity emerge into unity, the polygon into the circle.

But it's Reality, beyond duality, so even one's desire and will for this knowledge must be dropped at the door in order for one to cross it.[7] One does need his will – and all he has though in order to reach it – "so don't drop it too fast!"

– Thus Spoke Zarathustra's Son

*****

Time, as was mentioned above, is perceived by the occurrence of events [the nothing-something-nothing phenomena].

When the mind becomes, say, stressed, it becomes extremely alert (as when it senses and is trying to work out the correct "Fight or Flight" response[8]), and it perceives a lot of things or events closely on top of each other.

We may try to correlate our sense of time with the steady click or beat of the clock on the wall, but with all the perceptions being experienced as we try to calculate whether to fight or to fly, the correlation breaks down.

Our minds calculate all those perceptions, and translate that number [of perceptions] to our normal experiences in life – so what could have been 5 minutes of perceptions is really only 30 seconds on Newton's clock.

*****

And then there is Virginia Woolf, where all time, all life, and the Universe are merged into one point in time: "The Moment".[9]

> [For a parallel thought, please see Thomas Merton [in "2 PK's"] who instead uses the term "Contemplation".]

----

[7] See, for example, Thomas Merton:

So that the contemplative [a person or a monk] is at the same time question and answer.

. . .

Though these are two distinct and enormously different levels, yet they are in fact an awareness of the same thing. The question is itself the answer and we ourselves are both. But we cannot know this until we have moved into the second kind of awareness. We awaken not to find an answer absolutely distinct from the question but to realize that the question is its own answer and all is summed up in one awareness, not as a proposition but as an experience.

(For a more complete exposition of his thought, see Thomas Merton in "2 PK's".)

[8] You know the theory: you have milliseconds to determine how you are going to respond to a situation that will most likely end your life in the next few seconds [*if not sooner*]. Also see, e.g., "Silvertip Grizzly With Spirit Dog" and "Drunken Indian".

[9] Also see "Flickering Flames".

And "finally" there are the Wu Li Masters, ancient Chinese physicists, who saw the Universe as in a constant state of flux – who saw the rise, fall, changes and erosion of mountains as an expression of the "life" of the mountain (and thus, as another expression of the life of the Universe) [and, of course, following on that thought, mountains are neither "dead" nor "lifeless"].[10]

II

A New Theory on the Common Housefly

This of course now all leads to a New Theory on the Common Housefly.

What we call "houseflies" have been here on earth for millions of years.

That is, millions of years before houses, and millions of years before man. That gives them a very long head start.

One of the things that perplexed me when I was a kid was how an annoying housefly in my bedroom would disappear as I tried to get it (i.e., kill it).

Minutes later it would reappear, buzzing around me, and annoying the heck out of me.

The question that naturally arose was: where did it go?

Of course, now that we are all familiar with "Star Trek", it is conceivable – with millions of years as a head start – houseflies have developed a "cloaking technology" which allow them to fly around us undetected and undetectable until they decide to "uncloak", at which time they reappear and become an instant nuisance again.

That's possible.

But in light of Ouspensky's analogy about dimensions and time, it is also possible that these simple houseflies are just going off into other dimensions [mathematicians can now calculate out to the 9th or 10th dimension, while physicists insist they need 11 dimensions to explain the Universe (but what that looks like I have no clue as I am still moored down to just perceiving 3 dimensions)], only to return to buzz around and annoy us some more.

Just a thought.

---

[10] See "Geologic Time".

About the Author (Chief No Feathers)

Chief No Feathers & His Loyal Scout Muddy Paws

At the end of the Indian Wars out West, photographers from the East went out to photograph a disappearing way of life, if not quite a disappearing people.

[I have always known this photograph existed –

I had just never seen it before now.]

Sioux encampment[11]

---

[11] Can you tell which way the prevailing wind is blowing?

I saw this with seagulls in a parking lot in Delaware over a century later (except the seagulls were facing *into* the wind).

The Sioux have their smoke flaps set so that the smoke from the fires within their tipis (to keep them warm and to cook their food), [and so that the drafts for those fires are better and stronger] . . . blows away from their camp.

The "savages" at least knew what they were doing.

Some of the photographers concentrated on the people, their tipis and their camps, while others concentrated on taking portraits of their chiefs.

One of these portraits was of Chief Two Feathers.

I have no idea who Chief Two Feathers was, what his claim to fame might have been, or how he might have earned the two feathers. All I know is that there is a photograph of him.

*****

While working for the Tribe at the Fort, I was severely injured, with the injury requiring major surgery. When I went back about a week later to have the stitches removed from the various incisions, I was talking to the assistant surgeon. He asked what I did. I said I was the Executive Director of a tribe, but I didn't know if I was the Chief non-chief, or a non-chief Chief.

The surgeon, earlier in his career, like many doctors in Alaska, had worked out in the Bush in various villages, and knew of the tenuous and fluctuating reality of tribal power. I told him that while the staff and tribal members preferred to call me "Boss" [their term – not a term of my choosing], that there were real, but unspoken, limits to my authority.

~ Oh, said the surgeon, so you're like a chief with no feathers.

— Exactly – Chief No Feathers!

*****

Little Miss Bella has just put her right front paw on Captain Sparky's back, so he is about to react. (Blue huckleberries can be seen just behind Captain Sparky's tail.)

Golden colored fish can be seen in the pond behind the puppies. (They were all subsequently wiped out by being eaten by Snapping Turtles [see "The Prehistoric Creature With The Dinosaur Tail"].)

I had several projects going on at the Lower Pond, including building a dam to raise the water level of the pond, and a deck (see above) so we could go out over the pond and look down at the fish swimming by below. Captain Sparky and Little Miss Bella would be out there with me while I worked and they played. Shih Tzu's are not water dogs like Spaniels, so do not go out to swim. But they do recognize water for the purposes of drinking, and freely did so. While Little Miss Bella could do so without getting all messy, Sparky had a way of always finding the mud – hence his well-earned nickname: "Muddy Paws".

So when it was time for a break, and we'd go out to explore the forest, it was Chief No Feathers and his loyal scout Muddy Paws who went out with Little Miss Bella to see what the forest had in store for us that day.